M000289602

Pincushions

60 CROSS STITCH DESIGNS BY LINDA GILLUM

GENERAL INSTRUCTIONS

Working With Charts

How To Read Charts: Each design is shown in chart form. Each symbol square on the charts represents one Cross Stitch. A small symbol represents a Quarter Cross Stitch. Colored dots represent French Knots. The straight lines on the charts indicate Backstitch. Complete the Cross Stitches and 1/4 Cross Stitches before working Backstitches, Straight Stitches, and French Knots.

Symbol Key: The symbol key indicates the color of floss to use for each stitch on the chart. Symbol key columns should be read vertically and horizontally to determine type of stitch and floss color. The following headings are given:

DMC — DMC color number
X — Cross Stitch
1/4 — Quarter Cross Stitch
BS — Backstitch
FK — French Knot
Str — Straight Stitch

Counted Cross Stitch (X): Work one Cross Stitch to correspond to each symbol square on the chart. For horizontal rows, work stitches in two journeys (Fig. 1). For vertical rows, complete each stitch as shown (Fig. 2).

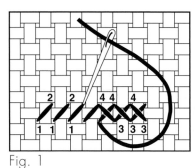

Fig. 1

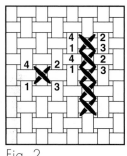

Fig. 2

Quarter Stitch (1/4): Quarter Stitches are denoted by smaller symbols on the chart and on the symbol key. Come up at 1, then split fabric thread to go down at 2 (Fig. 3).

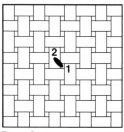

Fig. 3

Straight Stitch (Str): Work this stitch (Fig. 4) after the design has been completed.

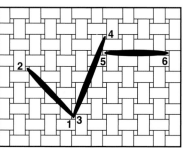

Fig. 4

Backstitch (BS): For outline detail, Backstitch (shown on chart and on symbol key by colored straight lines) should be worked after the design has been completed (Fig. 5). Stitch with one strand of floss unless otherwise instructed. When the chart shows a Backstitch crossing a symbol square, a Cross Stitch (Fig. 1 or 2) should be worked first, then the Backstitch should be worked on top of the Cross Stitch.

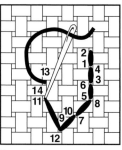

Fig. 5

2

French Knot (FK): Bring needle up at 1. Wrap floss once around needle and insert needle at 2, holding end of floss with non-stitching fingers (Fig. 6). Tighten knot, then pull needle through fabric, holding floss until it must be released. Stitch with one strand of floss unless otherwise instructed. For larger knot, use more strands; wrap only once.

Fig. 6

Stitching Tips

Preparing Fabric

Cut fabric desired size, allowing at least a 3" margin around the design. Overcast raw edges. It is better to waste a little fabric than to come up short after hours of stitching!

Working with Floss

To ensure smoother stitches, separate strands and realign them before threading needle. Keep stitching tension consistent. Begin and end floss by running under several stitches on back; never tie knots.

Dye Lot Variation

It is important to buy all of the floss you need to complete your project from the same dye lot. Although variations in color may be slight, when flosses from two different dye lots are held together, the variation is usually apparent on a stitched piece.

Where to Start

The horizontal and vertical centers of each charted design are shown by arrows. You may start at any point on the charted design, but be sure the design will be centered on the fabric. Locate the center of fabric by folding in half, top to bottom and again left to right. On the charted design, count the number of squares (stitches) from the center of the chart to where you wish to start. Then from the fabric's center, find your starting point by counting out the same number of fabric threads (stitches).

Note: Sizes of colored pictures do not correspond to sizes of designs in charts.

Finishing

ADHERING FUSIBLE BACKING

For best results we recommend Therm O Web Heat 'n Bond Ultra Hold iron-on adhesive which is available at your local fabric store. Follow manufacturer's instructions for permanent fusion, except do not prewash the fabric. Pre-heat a dry iron to silk setting. Place the fusible backing paper side up on the wrong side of the fabric. Glide the iron lightly over the paper for 1–2 seconds. Allow to cool. Cut project to size. Peel off the paper backing. With adhesive side down, center project on item or felt and iron for 4–8 seconds until bonded.

PROJECT INSTRUCTIONS

Flower Pincushions

MATERIALS

Cross stitched design
2–4" x 4" felt pieces (one for flower, one to cover bottom)
Cardboard
2" x 6" felt piece (for base)
¾" x 6" felt strip (trim around stitched piece)
Beacon Fabri-Tac Permanent Adhesive
Stuffing

INSTRUCTIONS

1. TOP: Cut stitched piece to make a 3½" circle, keeping design centered. Gather, stuff, and place on top of a 1⅜" cardboard circle. Pull to gather snugly. Tie off.

2. Stitch ends of ¾" x 6" strip together using a ¼" seam allowance. Fold in half lengthwise with wrong sides together and place around stitched piece to create edge. See photos. Slip stitch in place. Cut out flower shape using pattern on page 47 and place finished top in center, making sure the edges of trim are tucked under. Stitch in place.

3. BASE: Cut 3–1¾" circles of cardboard. Sew ends of 2" x 6" felt strip together, using a ¼" seam allowance. Turn right side out, gather one edge over 1¾" cardboard circle and tie off. Add stuffing and gather top edge of base. Place a cardboard circle on top of stuffing, pull gathers, and tie off. Cut a 2½" circle of felt, add a running stitch around edge and gather over remaining cardboard circle. Pull snugly and tie off. Attach to base with slip stitch.

4. Attach top of pincushion to base using a slip stitch.

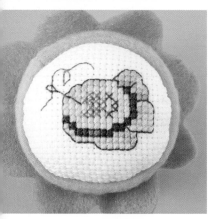

ALTERNATIVE IDEAS

Leaving off base of pincushion, attach the flower top to a strip of felt with a hook and loop closure at the ends to create a wrist pincushion. Or add one or two larger flower shapes under the flower top for a mini pincushion.

Charts on pages 21–22

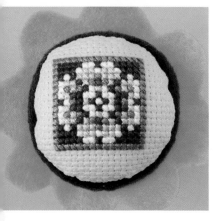

Hanging Pincushions

MATERIALS

Cross stitched design
3¾" round paper mache hanging ornament
Acrylic paint (opt.)
1¼" x 36" felt strip
⁷⁄₁₆" x 12" felt strip (opt.)
3¾" cardboard circle
Layered batting or stuffing
Beacon Fabri-Tac Permanent Adhesive

INSTRUCTIONS

1. Paint back and sides of ornament desired color or later cover edge with felt.

2. Cut stitched piece 5¾" round, keeping design centered.

3. Cut batting to slightly larger than 3¾" cardboard circle and place on top. Add running stitch around stitched piece and gather around batting and cardboard. Pull snugly and tie off.

4. RUFFLE: Stitch ends of 36" felt strip together and add running stitch along one side; gather to fit under base of stitched piece. Stitch in place to secure to stitched piece.

5. Glue finished piece to ornament with hanger at top. If you want a longer hanger, remove ornament hanger and replace with ribbon or cord before gluing pincushion together.

6. Glue the 12" felt strip around the edge of the ornament starting at the hanger.

Charts on pages 22-23

6

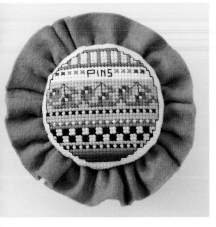

Round Box Pincushions

MATERIALS

Cross stitched design
2¾" round paper mache craft box
Acrylic paint
2¼" cardboard circle
1¼" x 18" felt strip
Layered batting or stuffing
Beacon Fabri-Tac Permanent Adhesive

INSTRUCTIONS

1. Paint paper mache box desired color.
2. Cut stitched piece to make a 4" circle, keeping design centered. Cut batting slightly larger than cardboard circle and place on top. Add running stitch around stitched piece and place on top of batting and cardboard. Gather and tie off.
3. RUFFLE: Stitch ends of felt strip together, add running stitch along one edge and gather to fit under stitched piece. Sew ruffle to stitched piece using a slip stitch.
4. Center ruffled pincushion on top of box and glue in place.
Charts on pages 23–25

Diamond Pillow Pincushions

MATERIALS

Cross stitched design
3" x 3" felt square
2–4"x 4" felt squares
Stuffing

INSTRUCTIONS

1. TOP PILLOW: Cut stitched design 3" square, keeping design centered. Place 3" felt square on top of stitched piece. Sew together using ¼" seam and leaving an opening for turning. Trim seam edges and clip corners; turn right side out. Stuff and slip stitch opening closed.

2. BOTTOM PILLOW: Place 4" squares of felt together and machine stitch ⅜" from edge, creating a flanged edge. Leave an opening for stuffing. Stuff then sew opening closed.

3. Attach the two pillows together by running a very strong coordinating thread from the bottom pillow center through the top pillow center and back down again. Pull to tighten and tie off.

Charts on pages 25–27

Square Pillow Pincushions

MATERIALS
Cross stitched design
2–4" x 4" felt squares
3½" x 3½" felt square
Stuffing

INSTRUCTIONS
1. TOP PILLOW: Cut stitched design 3½" square, keeping design centered. Place 3½" felt square on top of stitched piece. Sew together using ¼" seam and leaving an opening for turning. Trim seam edges and clip corners; turn right side out. Stuff and slip stitch opening closed.

2. BOTTOM PILLOW: Place 4" squares of felt together and repeat to make bottom pillow. Place small pillow on top and run a very strong coordinating thread from the bottom pillow center through the top pillow center and back down again. Pull to tighten and tie off.

Charts on pages 28–30

Stylish Accessories
Pincushions

MATERIALS
Cross stitched design
2–6¾" x 4⅝" felt pieces
5¼" x 3⅝" felt piece
Stuffing
Beacon Fabri-Tac Permanent Adhesive
 (opt.)

INSTRUCTIONS
1. TOP PILLOW: Cut stitched design 5¼"
x 3⅝", keeping design centered. Place
same size felt piece on top of stitched
piece. Sew together using ¼" seam allowance leaving an opening for turning.
Trim seam edges and clip corners; turn
right side out. Stuff and slip stitch opening closed.

2. BOTTOM PILLOW: Place 6¾" x
4⅝" pieces of felt together and repeat
to make bottom pillow. Attach stitched
pillow by applying a dab of fabric
glue at each corner on the back or by
slip stitching.

Charts on pages 31–32

Wooden Spool Pincushions

MATERIALS
Cross stitched design
3¼" felt circle
1½" cardboard circle
Wooden craft spool, 1½" diameter, 2⅛" high
Stuffing
Beacon Fabri-Tac Permanent Adhesive
Fusible backing

INSTRUCTIONS
1. Add running stitch around edge of 3¼" felt circle and gather. Stuff tightly and place cardboard circle on top of stuffing; pull gathers snugly around cardboard. Tie off.
2. Spread a layer of glue on top of spool and press felt pincushion firmly in place. Allow to dry.
3. Apply an iron-on fusible backing to stitched piece to prevent edges from raveling. (See Adhering Fusible Backing on page 3.) Cut stitched piece to size, being sure to allow for an overlap at back edges. Wrap stitched piece around spool and use iron at back edge to adhere.
Charts on pages 32–34

Animal Pincushions

MATERIALS

Cross stitched design
8" x 10" felt piece (for body and head)
6" x 8" felt piece in contrasting color
Small scraps of felt (for stitched piece and base)
Beacon Fabri-Tac Permanent Adhesive
Stuffing
Cardboard
1½" x 1½" wood craft square
Black floss
Fusible backing

BASIC BODY INSTRUCTIONS

1. Using patterns on pages 46–47, cut out body and head from felt. Cut out cardboard base.
2. BASE OF BODY: Using contrasting color, cut out felt circle ½" larger than cardboard base and add running stitch around edge. Place cardboard on felt and pull to gather felt around cardboard. Tie off.
3. Add running stitch around edge of body shape and pull to gather; stuff and gather until body fits on top of base. Pin and stitch to base.
4. Add running stitch around edge of head shape and pull to gather. Using 6-ply black floss, stitch French knot eyes. See photo for placement. Stuff and pull up gathers. Tie off and place on top front of body. Stitch in place.
5. LEGS: Using same color as base, cut four strips of felt 1¼" x 6". Roll each one up keeping edges even. Roll firmly but not too tight; legs should be ¾" in diameter. Make four legs and glue together, keeping bottom edges even. Trim if necessary. Stitch or glue legs to base of body.
6. BASE OF PINCUSHION: Cut felt to fit wood craft square and glue to square. Allow to dry. Glue or stitch bottom of legs to covered square.

BEAR

1. Using patterns, cut out muzzle, ears, and tail from contrasting color felt.
2. Use black floss to stitch nose. Pin muzzle in place just under eyes. Slip stitch to head leaving a space to stuff. Stuff and slip stitch closed.
3. Pinch together base of each ear and tack to secure. Pin to head and stitch to attach.
4. Roll up strip of felt for tail; glue or stitch to hold. Pin to bear body and stitch to attach.

PIG

1. Using patterns, cut out ears and tail from contrasting color felt.
2. Using pattern, cut out two pieces of contrasting color felt for nose. Place together and roll up, slip stitch ends. Using 6-ply pink floss, insert needle at back of nose and make a French knot in front; repeat for other nostril. Place nose just under eyes and glue or stitch to attach.
3. Pinch together base of each ear and tack. Place on head and stitch to attach.
4. Tack end of tail to rear of body; twist and tack other end to hold.

ELEPHANT

1. Using patterns, cut out ears, tail, and trunk from contrasting color felt.
2. Pinch together bottom of each ear to create a fold and tack. Place ears on head and stitch to attach.
3. Roll up trunk lengthwise and slip stitch to hold. Fold up end of trunk about ¼" and tack to hold. Place trunk on head just under eyes and stitch to attach.
4. Make a knot in end of tail and stitch other end to body.

ATTACHING THE DESIGN

1. Choose a square, round, or rectangular shape design for pincushion using patterns.
2. Apply fusible backing (see Adhering Fusible Backing on page 3) to stitched design; cut to size. Cut felt to size, about ⅛" larger, and iron on stitched design. Place finished piece on back of animal and stitch in place.
Charts on pages 34–37

Oval Box Pincushions

MATERIALS

Cross stitched design
5½" x 4" oval wooden box with recessed area in top
Cardboard
Layered batting
Beacon Fabri-Tac Permanent Adhesive

INSTRUCTIONS

1. Paint box desired color.
2. Trace oval inset area on top of box and make pattern to fit. Cut cardboard to size. Add ½" around pattern and cut out stitched design, keeping design centered.
3. Cut layered batting slightly larger than cardboard. Add running stitch around outside of stitched piece and gather, placing over batting and cardboard. Pull snugly and tie off. Place pincushion into recessed area on top of box and glue in place.
4. A box with a flat top can also be used. Glue the finished piece on top of box and add trim to edge.

Charts on pages 38–39

Sewing Box Pincushion

MATERIALS

Cross stitched design

6½" x 4⅛" wooden box with 4¼" x 2¼" opening in top. (We used one with screen in the opening, which was removed) OR, use a wooden box with no opening and place pincushion on top.

Acrylic paint

Cardboard

Beacon Fabri-Tac Permanent Adhesive

Layered batting or stuffing

Acid-free tape

Scrap felt or fabric

INSTRUCTIONS

1. Cut cardboard to fit opening (ours was 4¼" x 2¼") or cut to desired size if using box with no opening. Cut stitched piece 1½" larger on each side than cardboard. Cut layered batting slightly larger than cardboard and place on top. Place stitched piece on top of batting and fold around cardboard, holding in place with tape.

2. Place stitched piece over top of opening and adjust to fit, if necessary, by pulling away the tape and gently pulling the fabric, then tape to hold. Remove pincushion, add line of glue on inside of opening and place stitched piece in opening. Tape from underneath and cover exposed area on inside of lid with felt or fabric.

3. If using a box with no opening, glue finished pincushion to top and add trim to finish edge, if necessary.

Charts on pages 39–40

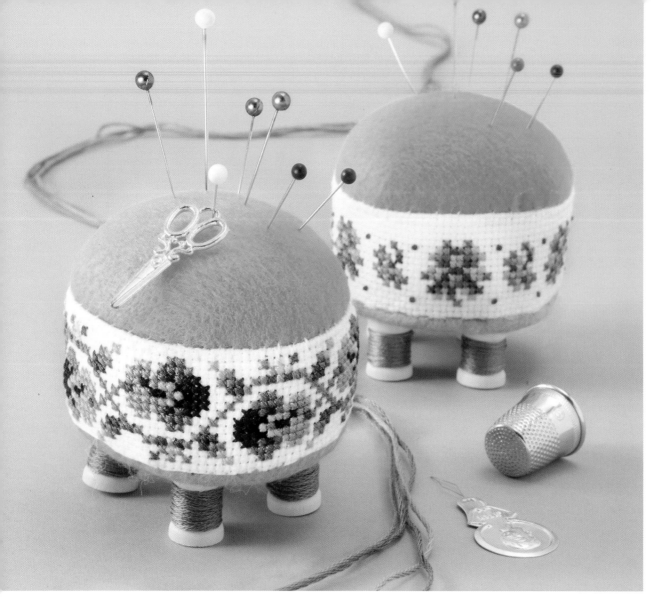

Spool Feet Pincushions

MATERIALS

Cross stitched design
4 wooden craft spools, ½" diameter, ⅝" high
Floss for wrapping spools
9" x 2" white felt strip
6" felt circle
3½" felt circle
2½" cardboard circle
Beacon Fabri-Tac Permanent Adhesive
Fusible backing
Stuffing

INSTRUCTIONS

1. BASE: Gather edge of 3½" felt circle and stretch over cardboard circle. Pull snugly and tie off. Wrap four spools with coordinating floss. Mark placement for spool feet on bottom of covered cardboard and cut out a small circle of felt at each spot. Glue feet directly to cardboard.

2. TOP: Gather the edge of the 6" felt circle and stuff. Pull gathers together to fit base. Tie off. Spread a layer of fabric glue on top of base and press felt puff firmly to base. Allow to dry.

3. BORDER: Use fusible backing to attach stitched piece to white felt strip. (See Adhering Fusible Backing on page 3.) Cut to size, making sure there is enough length to overlap at ends. Pin one end at back of puff with lengthwise edge even with base. Pull strip firmly around puff and pin to other end. Trim if necessary and stitch ends together.

Slip stitch along edges if necessary.

Charts on pages 41

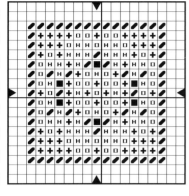

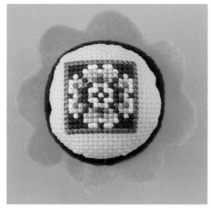

Blue Flower 15w x 15h

Design stitched on 14 count Charles Craft Lemon Twist using 3 strands for cross stitch.

DMC	X	Strands
white	▫	3
334	◢	3
797	✚	3
800	H	3
825	■	3

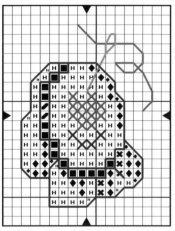

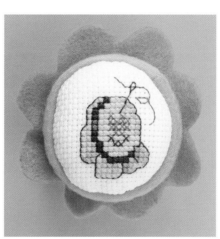

Cross Stitch 14w x 19h

Design stitched on 14 count Charles Craft White Aida using 3 strands for cross stitch, 1 strand for backstitching, 1 strand for French knots.

DMC	X	1/4	BS	Strands
335			◢	1
535			◢	1
738	◆	◆		3
839	■			3
839			◢	1
951	H	H		3
977	✖			3
3863	◢			3

Bee 9w x 9h

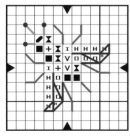

DMC	X	1/4	BS	FK	Strands	DMC	X	1/4	BS	FK	Strands
white	▫				3	743	V				3
310	■				3	793			◢		1
341	I				3	844	✖				3
435	◢				3	844			◢		1
435		◢			2	3811	H	H			3
435				●	1	3854	✚				3

Design stitched on 14 count Charles Craft White Aida using 3 strands for cross stitch, 1 & 2 strands for backstitching, 1 strand for French knots.

Tomato Pincushion 16w x 14h

DMC	X	1/4	BS	FK	Strands
304	⬆	↑			3
304			▨		1
310			▨		1
471	✚				3
666	♥	♥			3
742				⊙	1
946	△	△			3
971	H				3
3345	◆				3
3345			▨		1

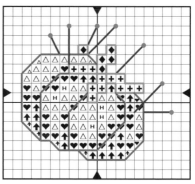

Design stitched on 14 count Charles Craft White Aida using 3 strands for cross stitch, 1 strand for backstitching, 1 strand for French knots.

Bless Our Home 39w x 53h
(Includes alphabet)

DMC	X	BS	Strands	DMC	X	BS	Strands
310	■		3	801	◢		3
310		▨	1	930	⬆		3
414	V		3	930		▨	1
666	♥		3	932	I		3
676	H		3	3346	✖		3
704	L		3	3346		▨	1
782	◆		3				

Design stitched on 14 count Charles Craft White Aida using 3 strands for cross stitch, 1 strand for backstitching.

Sampler 33w x 36h

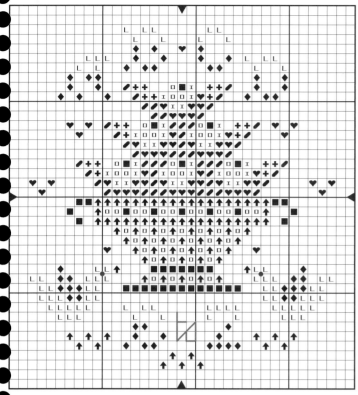

DMC	X	BS	FK	Strands
white	▫			3
347	♥			3
352	I			3
801	■			3
801			●	1
930	◆			3
930		╱		1
932	L			3
977	⬆			3
989	✚			3
3345	╱			3

Design stitched on 14 count Charles Craft White Aida using 3 strands for cross stitch, 1 strand for backstitching, 1 strand for French knots.

Yarn Basket 27w x 26h

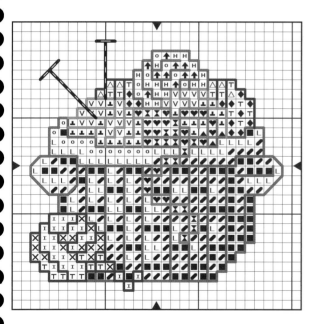

Design stitched on 14 count Charles Craft White Aida using 3 strands for cross stitch, 1 strand for backstitching, 1 strand for straight stitch.

DMC	X	BS	Str	Strands
333			╱	1
335	♥			3
335			╱	1
340	▲			3
341	⊥			3
369	I			3
535			✎	1
561	◆			3
561			╱	1
563	△			3
839	■			3
839			╱	1
912	T			3
951	○			3
957	⊠			3
977	H			3
3747	V			3
3813	⊠			3
3827	⬆			3
3863	╱			3
3864	L			3

Rose Monogram 42w x 64h

(Includes alphabet)

DMC	X	1/4	BS	Strands
335	♥			3
335			◪	1
816	■			3
899	✖			3
3041	◩			3
3326	△	△		3
3363	◆			3
3363			◪	1
3364	⊥			3
3727	I			3

Design stitched on 14 count Charles Craft
White Aida using 3 strands for cross stitch,
1 strand for backstitching.

Cosmos 30w x 30h

DMC	X	1/4	BS	FK	Strands
209	⊡	⊡			3
402	▲				3
604	♥	♥			3
605	H	H			3
818	○	○			3
3078	▣				3
3328	◆	◆			3
3328			◪		1
3688	◩	◩			3
3743	↑	↑			3
3799				◉	1
3803	■				3

Design stitched on 14 count Charles
Craft White Aida using 3 strands for
cross stitch, 1 strand for backstitching,
1 strand for French knots.

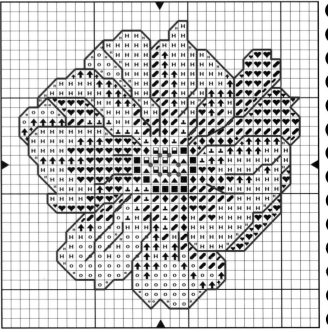

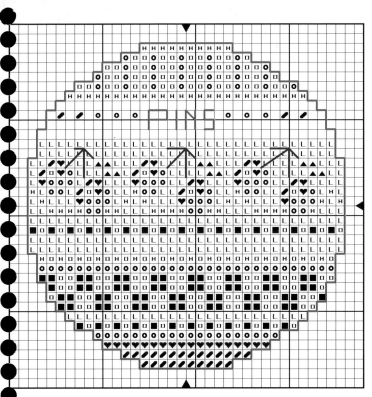

Pins 34w x 34h

DMC	X	BS	Strands
white	▢		3
310	■		3
310		◪	1
498	◪		3
666	♥		3
743	L		3
793	H		3
947	○		3
975		◪	1
989	▲		3

Design stitched on 14 count Charles Craft White Aida using 3 strands for cross stitch, 1 strand for backstitching.

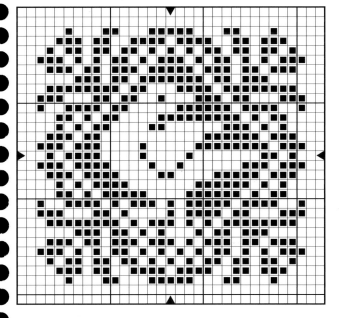

Tapestry Bird 29w x 27h

DMC	X	Strands
312	■	3

Design stitched on 14 count Charles Craft White Aida using 3 strands for cross stitch.

Flip Flops 27w x 21h

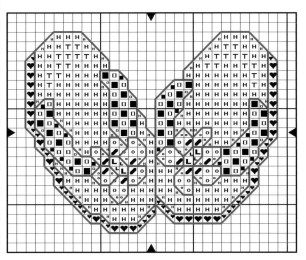

DMC	X	1/4	BS	Strands
white	▢	▫		3
310	■	▪		3
310			◪	1
742	L	∟		3
956	♥	♥		3
957	H	ʜ		3
963	T			3
3844	◪			3
3846	○	○		3

Design stitched on 14 count Charles Craft Lemon Twist Aida using 3 strands for cross stitch, 1 strand for backstitching.

White Rose 28w x 26h

DMC	X	1/4	BS	Strands
white	⊡	⊡		3
471	■			3
472	T	T		3
535			◤	1
743	H	H		3
744	○			3
945	⊠			3
3072	▣	▣		3
3346			◢	1
3687	♥	♥		3
3688	△			3
3826	◆			3
3826			◢	1

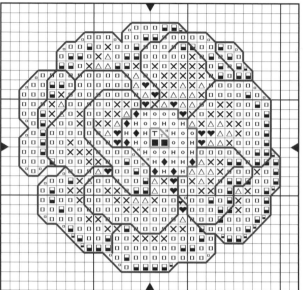

Design stitched on 14 count Charles Craft
Lt Green Aida using 3 strands for cross
stitch, 1 strand for backstitching, 1 strand
for French knots.

Flower Vase 29w x 29h

DMC	X	Strands
223	I	3
319	⊠	3
320	H	3
420	■	3
676	Z	3
813	⊠	3
825	◤	3
3721	♥	3

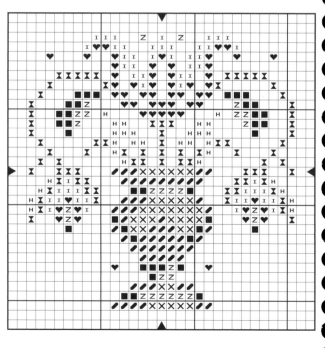

Design stitched on 14 count Charles Craft White
Aida using 3 strands for cross stitch.

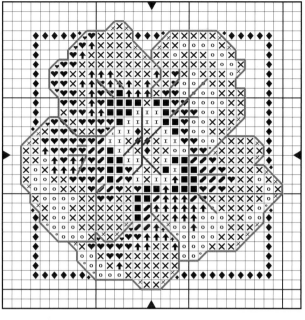

Nasturtium 28w x 28h

DMC	X	1/4	BS	Strands
300			◩	1
721	⊠	⊠		3
722	⊙	⊙		3
900	♥	♥		3
3328	⬆	⬆		3
3363	◆	◆		3
3363			◩	1
3799	■			3
3803	◪			3
3827	I	I		3

Design stitched on 14 count Charles Craft White Aida using 3 strands for cross stitch, 1 strand for backstitching.

Stars 'n Moon 28w x 26h

Design stitched on 14 count Charles Craft White Aida using 3 strands for cross stitch, 1 strand for backstitching.

DMC	X	1/4	BS	Strands
720	◆			3
741	●			3
742	⊥			3
744	⊙	⊙		3
794	H	H		3
798	■			3
798			◩	1

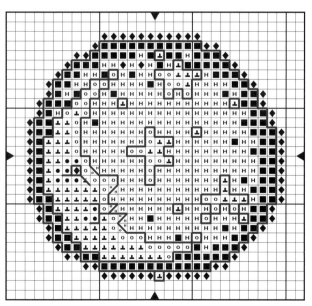

Pomegranate 40w x 35h

DMC	X	1/4	BS	Strands	DMC	X	1/4	BS	Strands
300	◆		◆	3	666	♥		♥	3
300		╱		1	739	△		△	3
312	✚		✛	3	975	◢		◿	3
312		╱		1	3363	↑		↑	3
352	○		°	3	3364	L		L	3
498	●		•	3	3371	■		■	3
520	✖		✗	3	3705	I		I	3
520		╱		1	3772	T		T	3

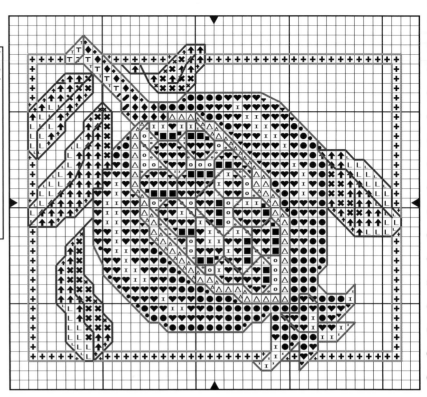

Design stitched on 14 count Charles Craft White Aida using 3 strands for cross stitch, 1 strand for backstitching.

Country Couple 37w x 39h

DMC	X	BS	FK	Strands	DMC	X	BS	FK	Strands
223	T			3	535	▲			3
223		╱		1	647	H			3
310	■			3	676	◉			3
310			●	1	813	□			3
319	↑			3	825	◆			3
320	L			3	3721	♥			3
353	V			3	3721		╱	●	1
420	◢			3					

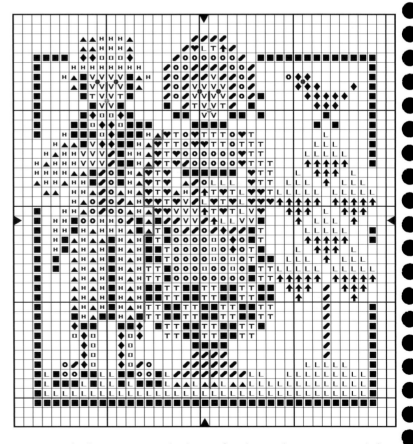

Design stitched on 14 count Charles Craft White Aida using 3 strands for cross stitch, 1 strand for backstitching, 1 strand for French knots.

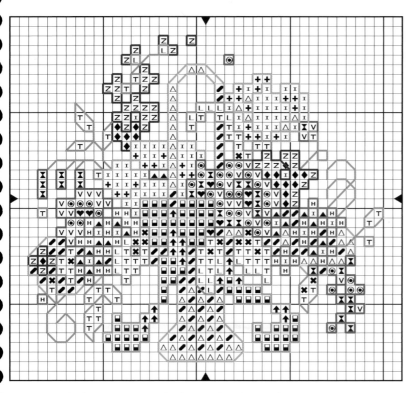

Design stitched on 14 count Charles Craft White Aida using 3 strands for cross stitch, 1 strand for backstitching.

Flower Basket 38w x 34h

DMC	X	BS	Strands	DMC	X	BS	Strands
208	▲		3	722	✚		3
208		╱	1	956	✕		3
210	H		3	957	◉		3
301	◢		3	959	⬆		3
301		╱	1	959		╱	1
304	♥		3	963	V		3
304		╱	1	964	▣		3
319		╱	1	989	T		3
334	◆		3	3325	Z		3
334		╱	1	3346	✖		3
369	L		3	3855	I		3
402	△		3				

Design stitched on 14 count Charles Craft White Aida using 3 strands for cross stitch, 1 strand for backstitching.

Fancy 37w x 37h

DMC	X	BS	Strands	DMC	X	BS	Strands
310	■		3	794	♥		3
535		╱	1	987	◢		3
677	L		3	989	I		3
729	✖		3	3607	⬆		3
793	H		3	3608	△		3

Sewing Machine 39w x 39h

DMC	X	BS	Str	Strands	DMC	X	BS	Str	Strands
208	✚			3	434	◩			3
211	L			3	742	⬆			3
310	◼			3	746	I			3
310		╱		1	783	◢			3
341	⊥			3	792	◆			3
350	♥			3	792			╱	1
413	4			3	793	✚			3
413		╱		1	989	H			3
414	✖			3	3824	o			3
415	I			3	3855	V			3

Design stitched on 14 count Charles Craft White Aida using 3 strands for cross stitch, 1 strand for backstitching, 1 strand for straight stitch.

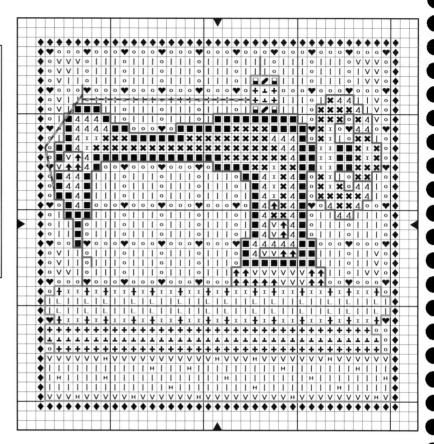

Heart and Checks 38w x 38h

DMC	X	BS	Strands	DMC	X	BS	Strands
white	◻		3	350	♥		3
310	◼		3	352	H		3
310		╱	1	3045	✖		3

Design stitched on 14 count Charles Craft White Aida using 3 strands for cross stitch, 1 strand for backstitching.

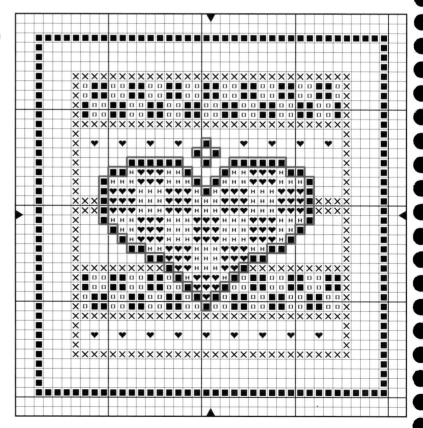

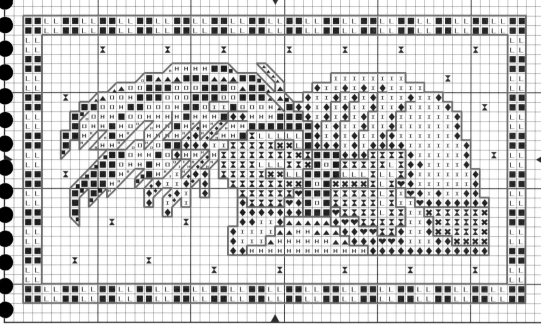

Pink Hat 54w x 30h

DMC	X	1/4	BS	Strands
white	□	□		3
310	■	▪		3
319	✖			3
321	♥			3
453	H	H		3
470	⧗			3
472	L			3
605	I	I		3
647	▲	▲		3
956	◆	◆		3
3799			╱	1

Design stitched on 14 count Charles Craft White Aida using 3 strands for cross stitch, 1 strand for backstitching.

Pink Purse 54w x 34h

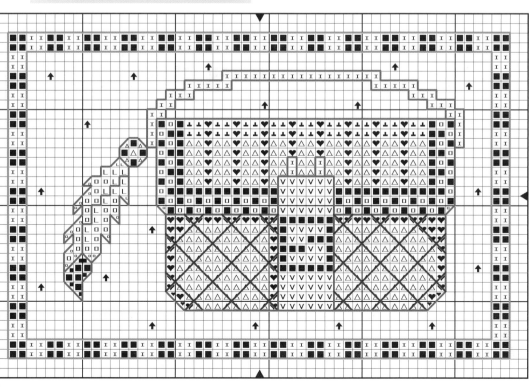

DMC	X	1/4	BS	Strands
100	□	□		3
310	■	▪		3
310			╱	1
321	♥	♥		3
453	L	L		3
471	V			3
728	I			3
816			╱	1
956	△	△		3
957	⊥			3
3799	↑			3
3799			╱	1

Design stitched on 14 count Charles Craft White Aida using 3 strands for cross stitch, 1 strand for backstitching.

Polka Dot Shoe 54w x 34h

DMC	X	1/4	BS	Strands
white	▢	▢		3
310	■	◼		3
321	✕			3
322	Z			3
453	T	T		3
535	▣	▣		3
535			╱	1
647	△	△		3
797	✕			1
813	╱			3
816	◆			3
956	✚			3
3799			╱	1

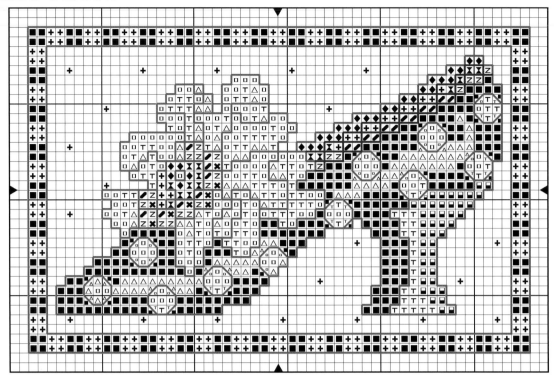

Design stitched on 14 count Charles Craft White Aida using 3 strands for cross stitch, 1 strand for backstitching.

Butterfly Border 57w x 21h

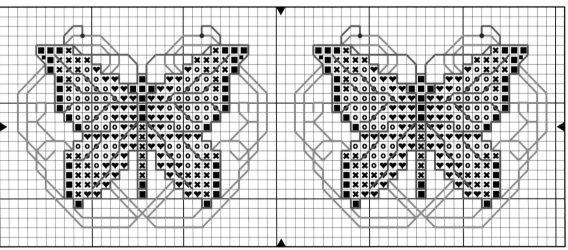

Design stitched on 14 count Charles Craft White Aida using 3 strands for cross stitch, 1 strand for backstitching, 1 strand for French knots.

DMC	X	1/4	BS	FK	Strands	DMC	X	1/4	BS	FK	Strands
210	♥				3	3053			╱		1
747	◎				3	3807	■	◾			3
794	✕				3	3807			╱	●	1

Rose Border 61w x 19h

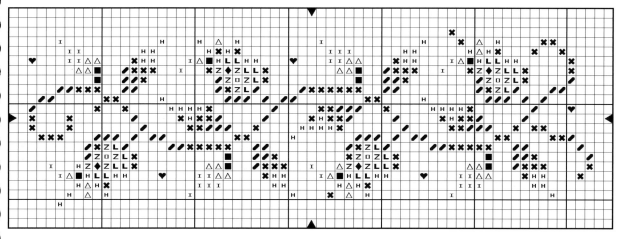

DMC	X	Strands	DMC	X	Strands
326	♥	3	899	Z	3
335	L	3	3326	□	3
471	H	3	3346	◢	3
502	△	3	3347	✖	3
814	◆	3	3813	I	3
890	■	3			

Design stitched on 14 count Charles Craft White Aida using 3 strands for cross stitch.

Old Rose Border 59w x 21h

Design stitched on 14 count Charles Craft White Aida using 3 strands for cross stitch.

DMC	X	Strands
223	✚	3
224	H	3
420	●	3
502	✖	3
503	△	3
561	⬆	3
729	□	3
744	I	3
913	o	3
989	T	3
3041	◆	3
3045	◢	3
3051	■	3
3726	♥	3

Grape Border 63w x 24h

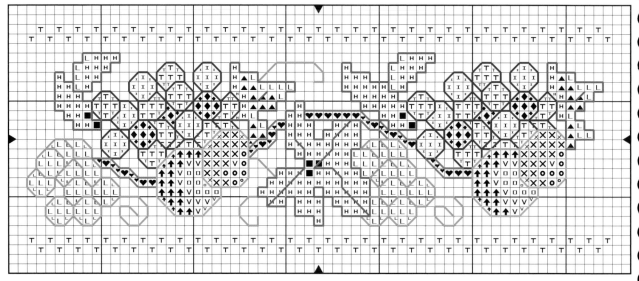

DMC	X	1/4	BS	Strands	DMC	X	1/4	BS	Strands
210	I	I		3	840	♥	♥		3
340	◆	◆		3	3051	■			3
402	◉	°		3	3051			╱	1
472	L	L		3	3053	H	H		3
550			╱	1	3053			╱	1
553	T	T		3	3776	⊠	⊠		3
704	▲	▲		3	3776			╱	1
745	□	□		3	3854	↑	↑		3
801			╱	1	3855	V	V		3

Design stitched on 14 count Charles Craft White Aida using 3 strands for cross stitch, 1 strand for backstitching.

Wild Rose 17w x 18h

DMC	X	BS	FK	Strands
white	□			3
368	◆			3
368		╱		1
472	I			3
743	⊠			3
745	T			3
957	♥			3
963	H			3
3726		╱	●	1

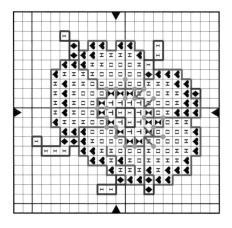

Design stitched on 14 count Charles Craft White Aida using 3 strands for cross stitch, 1 strand for backstitching, 1 strand for French knots.

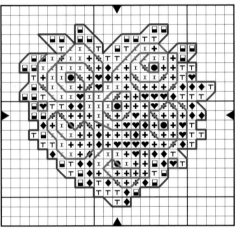

Bee Hive 22w x 17h

DMC	X	BS	Strands	DMC	X	BS	Strands
414		◪	1	3371	■		3
434	◪		3	3821	Ⅰ		3
435	⬆		3	3821		◪	1
898		◪	1	3852	◪		3

Design stitched on 14 count Charles Craft White Aida using 3 strands for cross stitch, 1 strand for backstitching.

Rose Bouquet 21w x 19h

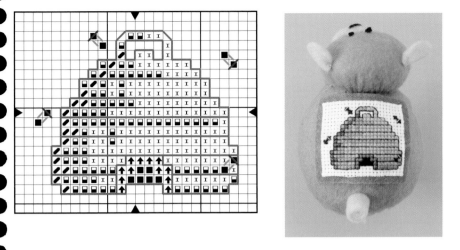

Design stitched on 14 count Charles Craft White Aida using 3 strands for cross stitch, 1 strand for backstitching.

DMC	X	BS	Strands
208	●		3
335	♥		3
335		◪	1
561	◆		3
561		◪	1
563	▣		3
912	T		3
957	✚		3
963	Ⅰ		3

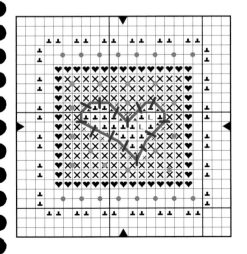

Patchwork Heart 19w x 19h

DMC	X	1/4	BS	FK	Strands
413			◪		1
956	♥				3
956			◪		1
957	⊥	⊡			3
957				●	1
963	L				3
3857	✕	⊠			3
3857				●	1

Design stitched on 14 count Charles Craft White Aida using 3 strands for cross stitch, 1 strand for backstitching, 1 strand for French Knots.

Rickrack Border 53w x 14h

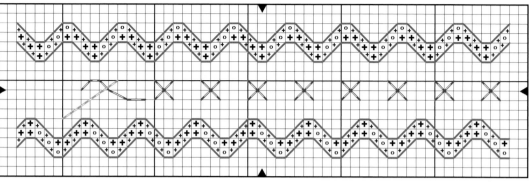

DMC	X	1/4	BS	Str	Strands
413				▧	1
413			▨		2
740			▨		2
742	✚	✚			3
743	○				3

Design stitched on 14 count Charles Craft White Aida using 3 strands for cross stitch, 1 strand for backstitching, 2 strands for straight stitch.

Cupcakes in a Row 52w x 17h

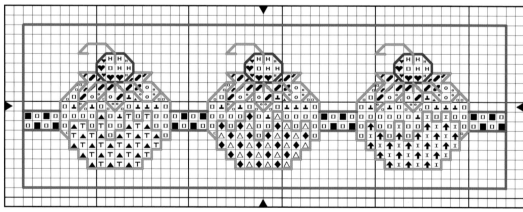

Design stitched on 14 count Charles Craft White Aida using 3 strands for cross stitch, 1 strand for backstitching.

DMC	X	1/4	BS	Strands	DMC	X	1/4	BS	Strands
white	▢	▫		3	798	⬆			3
209	△			3	809	I			3
310	■			3	815			▨	1
310			▨	1	956	▲			3
413			▨	1	963	T			3
608	H	H		3	966	○	○		3
666	♥	♥		3	3753	⬩	⬩		3
703	▨	▨		3	3837	◆			3

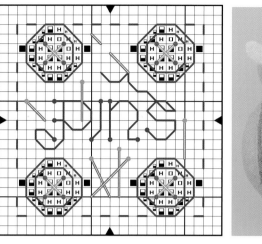

Buttons and Pins 20w x 20h

Design stitched on 14 count Charles Craft White Aida using 3 strands for cross stitch, 1 strand for back-stitching, 1 strand for French knots, 1 strand for straight stitch.

DMC	X	1/4	BS	SS	FK	Strands
white	▢					3
208				⟋		1
413	■					3
413			⟋	⟋	●	1
725					●	1
800	H	ᴴ				3
813	◲	⊡				3
824			⟋		●	1

Cupcake 12w x 13h

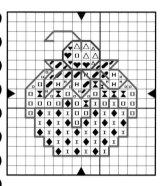

Design stitched on 14 count Charles Craft White Aida using 3 strands for cross stitch, 1 strand for backstitching.

DMC	X	1/4	BS	Strands
white	▢	⊡		3
413			⟋	1
608	△	△		3
666	♥	♥		3
703	◧	◪		3
815			⟋	1
956	◆			3
963	I			3
966	H	ᴴ		3
3753	✕	⊠		3

Pansy 24w x 21h

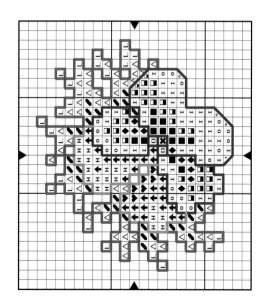

Design stitched on 14 count Charles Craft White Aida using 3 strands for cross stitch, 1 strand for backstitching.

DMC	X	1/4	BS	Strands
208	⬆			3
211	H			3
334	◆			3
334			⟋	1
369	L			3
743	▢			3
775	I	⊡		3
794	◼	◪		3
989	△	△		3
3346	◩			3
3346			⟋	1
3607	♥			3
3756	○	⊡		3
3799	■			3
3837			⟋	1
3854	✖			3

Garden Gate 58w x 42h

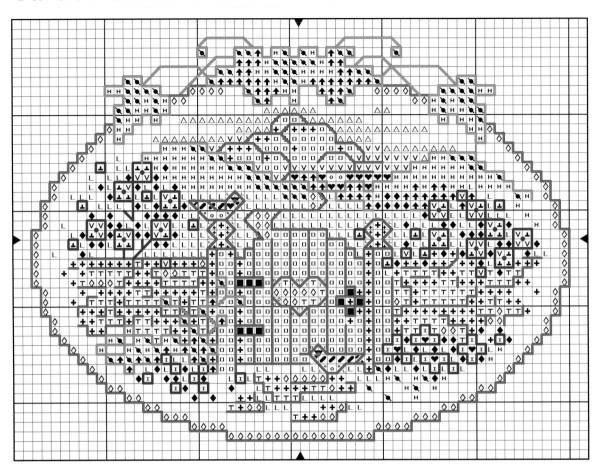

DMC	X	1/4	BS	FK	Strands	DMC	X	1/4	BS	FK	Strands
white	▫	▫			3	562	◣				3
310	◼				3	647	T	T			3
322	◩	◩			3	743	I				3
351	♥	♥			3	754	○	○			3
368	H				3	957	⬒				3
451	✚	+			3	963	V				3
472	L	L			3	3032	◇	◇			3
535			╱	●	1	3346	◆				3
561	⬆				3	3726			╱	●	1
561			╱		1	3811	△				3

Design stitched on 14 count Charles Craft White Aida
using 3 strands for cross stitch, 1 strand for backstitching, 1 strand for French knots.

Floral Border 111w x 10h

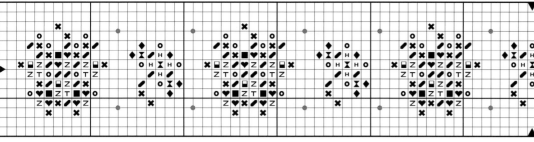

DMC	X	FK	Strands
334	◆		3
355		⊙	1
402	▣		3
745	T		3
800	H		3
809	✕		3
987	◢		3
988	✕		3
3348	○		3
3778	♥		3
3827	Z		3
3830	■		3

Design stitched on 14 count Charles Craft White Aida using 3 strands for cross stitch, 1 strand for French knots.

Pansy Border 111w x 13h

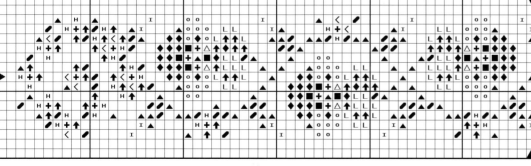

DMC	X	Strands
310	■	3
340	▲	3
341	L	3
472	I	3
501	◢	3
519	H	3
550	◆	3
553	○	3
743	✚	3
3347	▲	3
3811	‹	3
3854	△	3

Design stitched on 14 count Charles Craft White Aida using 3 strands for cross stitch.

Pink Rose with Border 30w x 28h

DMC	X	BS	FK	Strands
white	▢			3
335	♥			3
562	♠			3
562		╱		1
611	■			3
743	⊠			3
745	L			3
801		╱		1
957	⊥			3
963	○			3
3032	✚			3
3346	◆			3
3346		╱		1
3348	H			3
3726		╱	●	1

Design stitched on 14 count Charles Craft White Aida using 3 strands for cross stitch, 1 strand for backstitching, 1 strand for French knots.

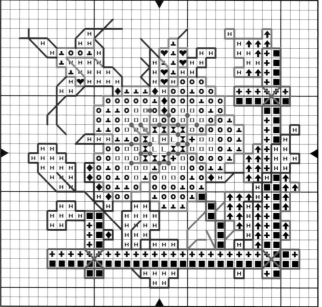

Watermelon 24w x 25h

DMC	X	BS	Strands
310	■		3
986	♠		3
986		╱	1
989	◣		3
3348	△		3
3731	♥		3
3733	H		3
3823	○		3

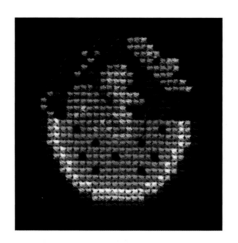

Design stitched on 14 count Charles Craft White Aida using 3 strands for cross stitch, 1 strand for backstitching.

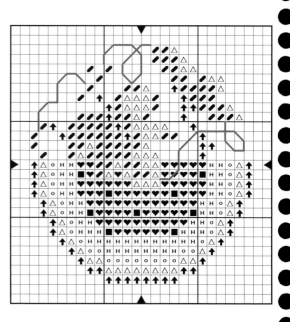

Lettuce 31w x 33h

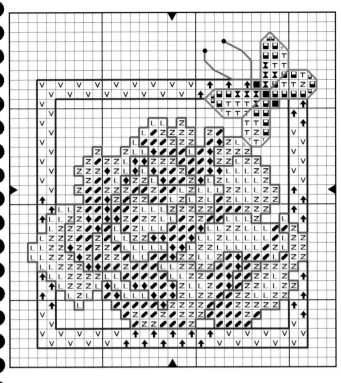

Design stitched on 14 count Charles Craft White Aida using 3 strands for cross stitch, 1 strand for backstitching, 1 strand for French knots.

DMC	X	1/4	BS	FK	Strands
209	⬆				3
211	V				3
319	◆				3
319			╱		1
327			╱		1
704	Z				3
743	▣	▫			3
745	T	T			3
772	L	L			3
919	■				3
919			╱		1
3346	╱				3
3776	✕				3
3799			╱	●	1

Teapot 29w x 18h

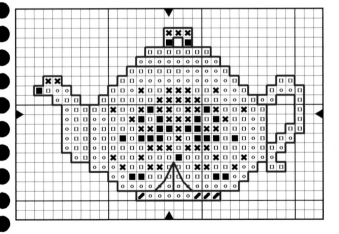

Design stitched on 14 count Charles Craft White Aida using 3 strands for cross stitch, 1 strand for backstitching.

DMC	X	BS	Strands
white	▢		3
322	✖		3
738	○		3
797	■		3
797		╱	1
3863	╱		3

Patchwork Quilt 26w x 26h

DMC	X	BS	Strands
310	■		3
310		◹	1
317	◊		1
602	♥		3
603	✕		3
605	I		3
704	✕		3
740	◆		3
741	H		3
743	T		3
3846	◢		3

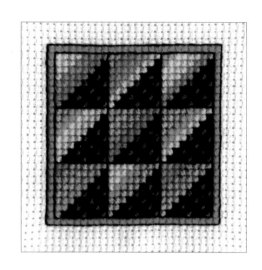

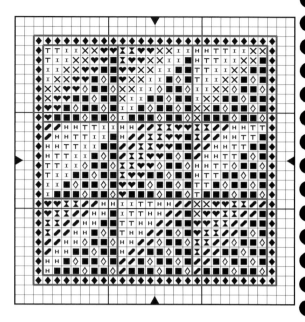

Design stitched on 14 count Charles Craft White Aida using 3 strands for cross stitch, 1 strand for backstitching.

Striped Shoe 44w x 30h

DMC	X	BS	Strands
white	▢		3
310	✕		3
321	◢		3
453	T		3
470	↑		3
471	L		3
647	◆		3
744	○		3
816	■		3
956	♥		3
3776	✖		3
3799		◹	1
3827	I		3

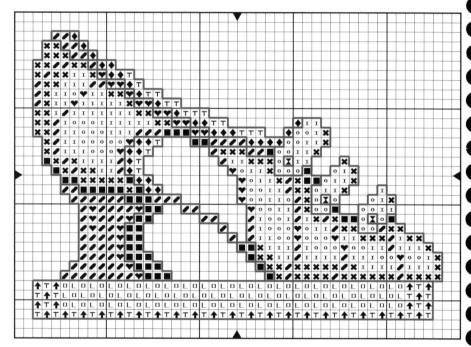

Design stitched on 14 count Charles Craft White Aida using 3 strands for cross stitch, 1 strand for backstitching.

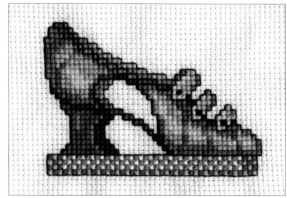

Stick It 17w x 22h

DMC	X	BS	Str	FK	Strands
white	▫				3
413	■				3
413			✎		2
666			◢	⊙	1
740	◆				3
740			◢	⊙	1
742	✚				3
742				⊙	1
3844			◢		1
3845	◢				3
3845				⊙	1

Design stitched on 14 count Charles Craft Grasshopper green Aida using 3 strands for cross stitch, 1 strand for backstitching, 1 strand for French knots, 2 strands for straight stitch.

Diamond Quilt 34w x 34h

DMC	X	Strands	DMC	X	Strands
310	■	3	3607	✖	3
519	L	3	3608	I	3
677	⊙	3	3807	◆	3
989	✚	3	3831	♥	3

Design stitched on 14 count Charles Craft White Aida using 3 strands for cross stitch.

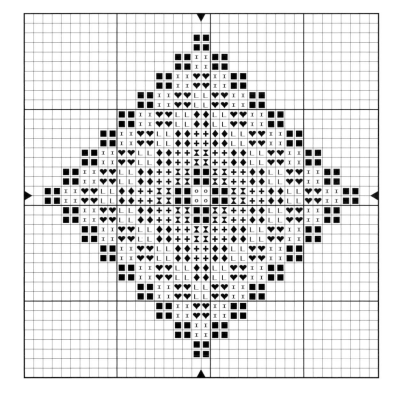

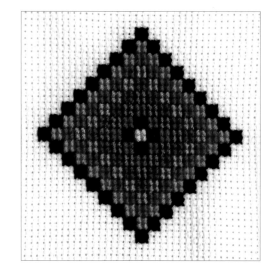

PATTERNS

ANIMAL PATTERNS

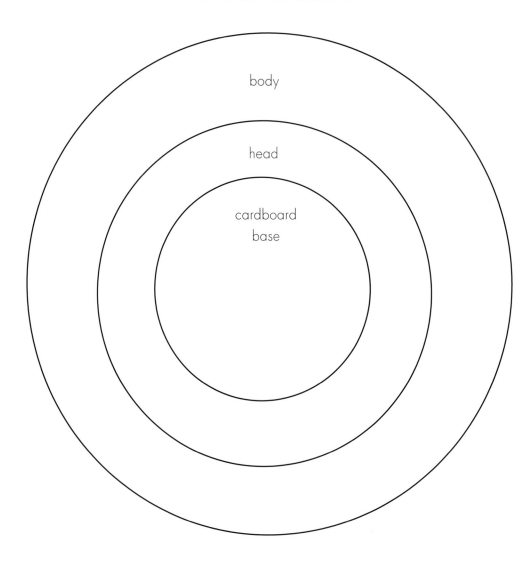

body

head

cardboard
base

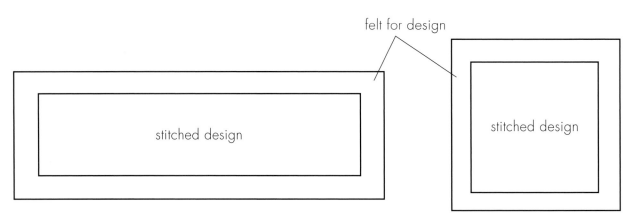

felt for design

stitched design

stitched design

PIG

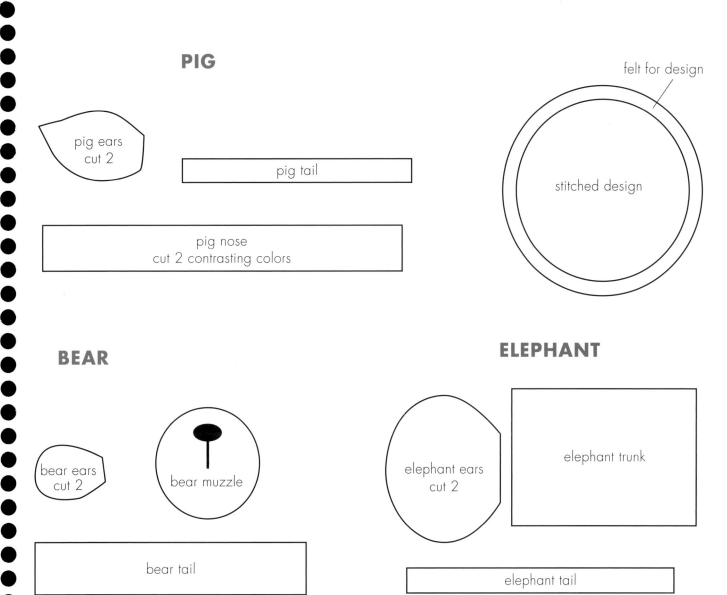

pig ears
cut 2

pig tail

pig nose
cut 2 contrasting colors

felt for design

stitched design

BEAR

bear ears
cut 2

bear muzzle

bear tail

ELEPHANT

elephant ears
cut 2

elephant trunk

elephant tail

FLOWER SHAPE

ARTIST

Linda Gillum

Linda Gillum, an award-winning needlework designer, is well-known for her coordinated baby ensembles, teddy bears, and her wonderfully realistic animals. She had authored numerous cross stitch and painting books and is a fine artist accomplished in oil pastels, as well as watercolor, acrylic, and oil painting. An avid animal lover, Linda is "mom" to two dogs and two cats and has enjoyed sharing her life with a host of other pets. Her humoristic approach and expert color skills have made her a popular designer with cross stitchers throughout the world.

Additional cross stitch projects by Barbara Baatz Hillman and Sandy Orton.

RESOURCES

Beacon Adhesives, Inc.
www.beaconcreates.com
125 MacQuesten Parkway South
Mt. Vernon, NY 10550
914-699-3405

KOOLER DESIGN STUDIO

Produced by:
Kooler Design Studio, Inc.
399 Taylor Blvd., Suite 104
Pleasant Hill, CA 94523
info@koolerdesign.com

Production Team:
- Creative Director: Donna Kooler
- Designers: Linda Gillum, Barbara Baatz Hillman, & Sandy Orton
- Editor-In-Chief: Judy Swager
- Technical Editor: Priscilla Timm
- Senior Graphic Designer: Ashley Rocha
- Photographer: Dianne Woods
- Art Director: Basha Kooler